ALL SUSPICIONS HAVE BEEN CONFIRMED

ALL SUSPICIONS HAVE BEEN CONFIRMED

SHANE STRANGE

All suspicions have been confirmed
Recent Work Press
Canberra, Australia

Copyright © Shane Strange, 2020

ISBN: 9780648834373 (paperback)

 A catalogue record for this book is available from the National Library of Australia

All rights reserved. This book is copyright. Except for private study, research, criticism or reviews as permitted under the Copyright Act, no part of this book may be reproduced, stored in a retrieval system, or transmitted in any form by any means without prior written permission. Enquiries should be addressed to the publisher.

Cover image: 'E. 8th st.' by James Jowers, 1967
Cover design: Recent Work Press
Set by Recent Work Press

recentworkpress.com

MD

For Ned

Contents

Everything, all the time	1
Anticipation	2
Eight ways to make fire	3
In other universes	6
A fluid measure	7
The order of things	8
OO	9
Space Invaders	10
The formula	11
Night	12
High country	13
Canberra	14
Japan	15
Near Kyoto station	16
Water falls	17
LBG	20
Rituals	21
Original shell	23
Abstraction	24
Uses of poetry 8	25
Sketches preparatory to an as yet unwritten children's book (1-3)	26
Portrait of the Queensland police officer as a young man	27
Apostles	28
Journey	29
Navigation	30
Andachtsbilder	31
Seafaring	33
Focus pulling	35
Flight	36
Spaceman Bones	37
The chapel astronomer	39

Everything, all the time

I wake to crisis.
The length of the world is unknown.
Birds fly and never return.
Each thing leaves and does not return.
The sun rises and succumbs to the horizon.
Names do not matter anymore.
Night breaks like an egg.

I tend a small fire.
The circle of light ends there,
Or does it begin,
lately converging on this point?

A dog will circle a fire three times
before laying down or leaving.
A star makes a circle in the sky.
Ashes rise toward the sky,
lifted by smoke.
Or do they fall?

And in the morning still the unanswered question.
A rumble in the earth that will not loosen stone.

Anticipation

Thelonius Monk brings his finger down and hooks a skin-stretch moment out to the boundaries like a kid's eyes closed waiting for his back to be drawn on by a fingernail or a wooden spoon to be brought down on bare upraised feet for what? Forgetting the 8 times table? Or because you woke up with blood in your ears you never hit me because I'd learned sneaky-wise to keep everything down in my guts but you made me watch while you did it. It could've happened to me you wanted me to know it could've happened to me and still can and old Thelonius with his finger in the air he knows how to borrow or maintain the blush. And it feels like that. But good.

Eight ways to make fire

1.
I watch him outside, in the cold morning. I watch as he braces his legs and raises the axe over his head and, with two arms, brings the axe down. In my mind's eye I can see the muscles flex and contract in his back, the tendons in his legs strain, the muscles on the side of his neck widen beneath his scarf. Mists roll in the valley. The mountain is covered in a grey veil. When the sun rises higher it will burn off the mists. Through the day, the shadow of the mountain will meander across the valley before darkness again.

2.
He is a big, slow man—the bear man. I am the tiny bird: the sparrow; the wren. I flutter. When he opens his arms, I fall into his paunch, and he wraps his arms around me folding his claws together at the nape of my neck.

3.
I imagine that he has become an adept, a scholar, a high priest of me: versed in my emotions. I should be grateful, but his levelness has been used, at times, in judgement of me. We have had mighty battles. No quarter has been given. More than once, we have verged on dissolution. In this way we have mapped our tendernesses.

4.
Some days we walk long into the property, him and me, tracing cattle tracks, noting rusted barbed wire fences and tiny gullies of eroded soil. There is a forest of eucalypt trees and low scrub down the mountain and into the valley. The trees are silent and shambolic, with gnarled branches tapering into the sky seeking fissures in the air.

5.
Once, we discovered an old house down beyond the forest. A solid, brick chimney stood alongside foundation stones: the outline of a home. Inside that area, he found an old tin can and a solid piece of rusty metal he said was a tool of some kind. Near the chimney I found the rim of an old pot, a china cup handle, a bone. I stuck my head inside the chimney. The back was stained dark— charred bricks crumbling. In a shadow in the back corner something shone for a moment and without thinking I reached my hand in to grasp the shiny thing. A tiny spoon, stained green and black, such as might be used to feed a child or a baby. 'Be careful,' I felt his hand between my shoulders. I stepped out and he pointed up to the top of the chimney where a brick teetered out over the edge, ready to fall. We walked back through the trees and along the cattle tracks in silence. He carried the metal tool with him, and I held the spoon in my pocket, secretly rubbing its bowl with my thumb.

6.
I make lunch, watching him working on the wood shed from the kitchen window. I watch him saw wood with a handsaw on an old wood horse, and drill nails with a hand drill, and sand down boards with sandpaper wrapped around an off cut block of wood. I know at the end of the day he will have exhausted himself, and I worry he overdoes it. But he is strong. At the table in the kitchen, we eat in silence.

7.
In the evenings, we eat on a small table in the lounge room. He clears the plates, washes the dishes while I sit in an armchair with a glass of wine, staring into the fire. I hear the chink and splash of dishes as he washes them in the water. He hums to himself while he cleans: croaky and low.

8.
The fire is like a hand holding me, and a hand crushing wood into bright embers. I can feel wine drawing down my throat like a long cold wire. White smoke is being drawn upwards into the chimney and across the mountain. It is the smoke that chokes us, never the fire. What is this place we are in?

In other universes

                     the parts actors play are their real lives. They don't know why they speak to themselves in dramatic monologue. The people you slept with have traded places with the people you wished you'd slept with. The dog you owned as a child appears on TV as a Sunday morning cartoon, beloved by children everywhere, and lives in the memory of adults as nostalgia warm and pure. Narrative time gawps at an empty plain and waits for movements of the sun. Unbroken attention spans hold on and hold on and hold on...

                     In other universes, each conclusion is the right one. All suspicions have been confirmed. Each decision has been made, each chance taken. Each possibility is achieved. Each sperm and egg are children. Each bomb dropped does not explode. Every indiscretion has been discovered. Every daydream lives and aches and draws pay. In other universes the molecules comprising the body differ by one. Cancer is good. Gods pray to humans, and humans pray to dust.

                     In other universes, the fears you wake to have manifested, or remain ideal. However, their sum never diminishes or expands. In all universes, this is a constant.

A fluid measure

Water always trickling in my ears like the leavings of a fountain. It pools in my eyes when I sleep. I step across empty baths in winter. I pick old bicycles from the river, and shopping trolleys, and rusted anchors from mud flats when the tide goes out. In summer I watch dragonflies hovering over stagnant ponds hoping they don't drown. Mother told me never to fill the bath above the knuckle of your finger. And a cup of water's all that's needed to wash the dinner plates. She drank from thimbles and trembled at waterfalls. We are mostly water, I told her one day. That made her shiver for a week. The rain gets in now, in the corner of the room, and the plaster is coming away from damp. I find my fingers pruning in dry air, a stream running down my back. I hear the ocean when I dream. The waves coming in and rolling over me and taking the smallest piece with them, again and again and again.

The order of things

The cows are obedient as they line up for the dip. Shitting in the mud where they stand, they move forward down the race: inch by inch to the edge. Two men with electric prods force the cows into the dipping trench: one by one by one. And the boy sees from the fence how they work as a machine: the line of cows; the men.

The dip itself is milky blue and splashes across the yard as each cow jumps in. When the boy gets some on his skin his grandfather tells him to 'wipe it off quick' with his red handkerchief. The boy does as he's told. 'Chemicals,' his grandfather mumbles. But the boy is more concerned about the red handkerchief, and the bull in the yard next door, waiting, he has been told, to be neutered.

OO

What was that inky stuff used to mark lines on primary school ovals? The plodding groundsman pushing a dispenser before sports day—scowling. (Where did they find these guys? A factory in Adelaide? An exporter in Hull?) The metal wheels creaking along the grass. (I can still hear the pre-plastic sound). I knew the lines because I sat behind them, watching the action take the field, run the line, circle the oval (twice for the 800m). There was no glory watching the crushed, greasy blades of grass; committing the earthy petroleum smell to memory; noting bulbous red ants fail to traverse the oily barrier. On this side of the line, bum sore from sitting, (and arm too, from playing 'punchies' with Mark Tyler) there was boredom enough to make slow observations. While over there the world went on in high speed confusion, never bothering time.

Space Invaders

In my mother's corner store,
where a burst bottle cut
a line through my thumb,
a pack of boymen came to play
'spacies', smoke on the path,
joke with my mother (firm on swearing,
but didn't mind a laugh) and change
dollar notes to coins for the machines.

Danger hung off them like waistcoats.
Stained with bruises and homemade tattoos,
they'd horde for position, a go, a turn.
Cowering in the back room, my brother and I
listened as they piled stories
as high as their scores.

Their mothers sent them alone
to buy bread as punishment
for not having work, for living at home.
Respecting the deal, my mother took
their mother's money stopping the change
being spent on raffle tickets, on smokes.

Sometimes, at closing,
with permission to slip a coin in, I'd look back
to watch my mother counting.
While my brother shot lines of lowering aliens,
I'd see behind her rows of cigarette packs:
unsold and safe in their homes, fading as it darkened
and evening evolved its own order.

The formula

We, I and an unnamed you, observe an object which is like an associated object, or feeling, or memory of a feeling, or a thing once observed in childhood. This is the first utterance—the baseline of experience.

I will expand on the discussion of the object, invoking an emotion or shades of an emotion, or the impossibility of emotion. I will try to imagine how you might see or experience the same object, though you will in fact have made no comment or indication you have any opinion at all. This is the second utterance.

Next will come a complication, perhaps you have made a point to which I don't agree, or I have stated my case too firmly, or I recall that my perceptions have changed completely from a younger self. This complication will open into a sustained simile, relating either to the object which opened the piece, or to point out the similarity between that object and the ways in which I have compared it to other objects, feelings or memories thus far.

At some point, you will do something minor into which I will read a great deal or nothing, either of which will be significant. At this point I will suggest, through the statement of seemingly unrelated conclusions, there has been a realisation of some kind.

The last utterance will be left open

Night

Youth is firing off
in the park. Dark laughter over
the sound of cars on the
arterial. Wave forms.

We lie in undress,
hot, meaty, wondering
if we will sleep our thoughts away
in youth maybe.

Or in roadsides. Or in gamey
others who traced
our bodies back then, when
we didn't know

each other. When we didn't think
it would end
up like this.
Not like this at all.

High country

The candle wax arms
of snow gums
like a precondition
for disease.
Peaks filed away
into cold war chalets.
Trees bleached
like coral,
like cemetery fingers.
Above the treeline:
cankerous boulders.
Winds shimmer,
thinly-pitched,
the waiting you.

Canberra

Spring breeze off drainage channels.
Four-lane roads taking
people away like a finger
wiping dust from a sill.
One could drive all night
to find a sky so blue. Yet,
here it is, in used car lots
and Pepsi cans:
the shale weight of the world
pressing down like a joke
and a promise—all at once.

Japan

1. Osaka to Kyoto

Soviet architecture finds its analogue along this railway line. No petering out into suburbs and fields. No dialectic of country and town. Expressways tangle like roots in the air with unrepentant tower blocks as graveyards in the sky. Wires segment clouds. Carriage windows fog in the cold. The mountains are green on the horizon, pegged down into earth by electricity pylons like two fingers pressed into the nape of a neck.

2. Saru, the monkey god, describes a laundromat in Kyoto.

Saru was able
to describe the moon,
What would he make
of this small room?
A room of moons? A need for change?
The folding away of smalls?

An old woman does sudoku.
The bodhisattva emerges,
splits her face in two.

3. Ceramics, Japan

A porcelain bowl on purple cloth. A milky blue eye at its base. A box to carry it in. All sensuous characteristics extinguished.

The meiping vase shaped like a lover's hip (celadon in pale blue, inlaid with crane and cloud) draws the eye but forbids the hand.

Near Kyoto station

I carried my postcard to you in the rain and the words washed away and the post office was closed. As I passed the Bar Populare the waiter stood inside the door watching a line of empty barstools against the wall. A crowd caught me on the corner and washed me in to some place under fluorescent lighting and it yelled at me like a storm, and I remembered my eyes were sore, and people were staring at phones because it was the only way they knew home. When I got out of that place and found my way back, I had nothing, not the smallest thing, to show for it. And I thought about you, and how you kept me warm, and how sorry I was I hadn't written

Water falls

1.

On the Chinese side,
a phalanx of trim hotel buildings
line a cliff at exactly 45 degrees from the falls.
Plump daddies with cameras like ordnance are pushed
around on neat punts, performing
tourist with novelty and national pride.

                      On this side—the side of Vietnam—
            rough paths cross a field past a buffalo tied;
a rusting tractor; two circular formations of hay squat:
      pre-industrial, ritualistic, necessary; punts of thick
                bamboo wound together with rough
                          jute rudimentary as breath.

2.

We stop before the falls, bobbing over the wash of other
craft. The boatman holds a cigarette in his teeth. The
wind blows fine embers to water.

I know the stick the boatman holds and pushes firmly into the soft
bed of the river is keeping me still against the current,
with his arms and chest, his legs and back,
the white flesh of his gripping hands.

The river does not know how it should be marked. It
only knows to flow and to fall and to meet the sea and to
rise again unmarked. Is that a kind of knowing? There is
no translation for the sound of water crashing on water
or lapping on bamboo—though these words are a kind
of translation.

Closer to the falls, the mist seeds water on my face,
a performance of tears to lie among other lies.

3.

The falls are calligraphy,
low like a fist grasping—

water breaching the knuckles,
falling like white linens.

A fisherman sits atop them
like an obligation, his rod addressed

where water meets air:
catching fish before they fly.

Girls embroider in market stalls
selling baby clothes and cheap toys.

I buy two magnetised stones that,
when thrown in the air,

attract to each other
with a satisfying 'clack'

Is that important?

LBG

A hand is like the earth.
Hold it upward and offer the sky
something of yourself.

A river is like the rain caught
in the palm of your hand.
It falls to the lowest point.

When it rains,
A roof, or a wall,
is like an explosion.

This lake is a dream of architects.
A pane of glass on the earth.
A sky falling to its lowest point.

Rituals

1.

We walk the picture through the sand, not following any footsteps but following the picture. We made you leader, giving you a pelican feather for your hair. We bury the picture half way and watch the shadow it casts from the sun's journey across the sky. At four points you must mark the shadow in the sand and later, at four points more. From these calculations we build the platform and the light. You stand on the platform. We dance in two circles. The knife is drawn across your neck. The light burns your shape into the platform. Your blood makes the picture. We lift it from the platform. We walk the picture through the sand.

2.

There's a reduction in the shadows going long and low. See! They crawl across the sand in the roughness made by sky and wave. Only babies—heading to sea for the first time. Pulling knives we cut until we find the one we want—the one with the pretty seed inside. There's always one and sometimes two. We cut through them all to be sure, leaving the beach full of little deady deads. Don't be sad and don't be blamey. That's the way it's done. Sort them, cut them, throw them away: a little reduction, in the shadows and other things.

3.

Time moves forward: each moment a brick upon the last. Tramping tight circles in the grass, we mimic birds on thermal winds above. I am surprised to meet you in this fruitless display. Your wings are bare, and you break each eye you meet against the roof of your mouth. You know how the story ends: the wasted hours; the ashes sifted from dry mouths; the papers piled high and left drying in corners. Why did I think this time would be different?

4.

In the garden there are eight paths: three for martyrs; two for lovers ; and one each for Mephisto, Loki and Death. In the centre of the garden, a chair made of ancient plumwood. Here the visitor is bound and asked to recite the verse from memory. There are traps in the recitation: sudden changes of meter, enticements to incorrect tone, self-important passages that must be spoken with humility, humble passages that must be sung, and a silence in the centre that can only be timed with breaths. It is at this point that one might fall asleep, dreaming of eight paths leading, like the branches of a plum tree, to forgetting, mischief, inconstancy, sophistry, the world serpent, the fen-dweller, mute children, or God.

Original shell

In the mind's eye, even this cardboard box is home. And not any home, but first home, safety home: the room that held us as an original shell.

We never forget the primitive urge to recline on stairwells; take refuge in passageways; rest against doors. All unfit for purpose, but indicative of a need to be still in places of transit, of movement, of egress.

We may glimpse the sky in echoes of crystal palaces, but never the horizon. Fear is quotidian, calcified, carapaced over the self until you are dug from the earth forever in recoil.

This is the wall, the floor, the ceiling. This is the box of memories: the original shell. This is the night time. Here comes the night time.

Abstraction

The alarm at 80 decibels. Carbonised bread, and coffee crystals dissolved in boiling water. Water pressure; textile manufacture; the combustion reaction. The ozone layer depleting at the same rate as dignity. Paper mills churn. Precious metals are extracted. Discard is studied for business cases and quality profiles. Houses stir and rise up across the land like kindly giants. The young confuse sincerity for depth. Bones are sold in marketplaces. Vows are taken. Rhythms find their way into incantations. Naked sticks are broken against each other. Stones are rolled into a circle. Somewhere flint is knapped into the head of a spear as it has been for 8, or 80, or 80,000 years.

Uses of poetry 8

You begin service in an unnamed base in the Nevada desert about an hour from Las Vegas. You fly unmanned airborne vehicles over countries in the Middle East and Africa with the purpose of making poetry of enemies of your country.

Due to time lags in the satellite connection, and the fog of war, it is rarely clear you have achieved the aim of any mission, and you are haunted by the growing suspicion you may have inadvertently made poetry of innocent civilians: children, the elderly, as they go about their everyday lives.

In time this suspicion turns into a neuroses that leads to an early (but honourable) discharge. Procedure dictates you are handed an envelope by your commanding officer. The envelope contains the number of poems you have either made, or assisted in being made through your actions. You suspect the number is large. You open the envelope.

Sketches preparatory to an as yet unwritten children's book (1-3)

Young Duck is getting ready for his first day at school. Mother Duck is quiet. 'Why are you quiet, Mother Duck?' asks Young Duck. 'Because' says Mother Duck 'I equate significant milestones in your life with the inevitable narrowing of opportunities in mine. It is unfair, I know, but I need a moment to retrieve myself from the existential angst that, if left festering, might consume me. (show illustration)

Junior Bear is helping Papa Bear. Together they are building a letterbox. Look at the letterbox. It is a red letter box. Junior Bear asks 'Papa Bear, why is the letterbox red?' 'Because, Junior Bear' begins Papa Bear 'in a class society my labour is alienated to the point where I can only show my resistance through meaningless symbols of solidarity that mask my tacit complicity with the system.' (show illustration)

It is a lovely day in the park. Little Iguana is flying a kite. Look at it soar! Baby Turtle is getting older. Look at her mature! Little Crocodile is playing with lipstick. Look at him experiment! Junior Panda knows she really likes girls. Look at her hiding! Papa and Papa Iguana are watching Little Iguana. Look at them overturn preconceptions! Little Baby Possum feels responsible for her parents' divorce. Look at her self-blaming! Daddy Ocelot feels weighed down by the tropes of masculinity. Look at him conform! It is a lovely day in the park. (show illustration)

Portrait of the Queensland police officer as a young man

To staunch the flow of blood
he would have to reverse the punch
and unhear the 'cunt' addressed to him
from the mouth of the man whose hands
were cuffed behind his back.
And, through a series of re-contortions,
unhandle that man's body and release him
into the back seat of the police car.
And he would have to watch that car reverse
up the street in front of the lock up
and return to the conversation with his Sergeant
who he would have to unhear saying
'No copper took shit from an Abo'.

And returning home he would have to de-dress
and stand, clean in his own skin,
pushing water into the shower's nozzle,
unthinking little affirmations,
re-applying his stubble,
walking backward down the hall,
decompressing muscle,
unfucking his fiance and
sliding into a coma from where
he would never remember.

Apostles

El Greco's apostles emerge from black
like half-dreams of colour.
These are not the father, or the son,
but the holy ghost: ascetic faces;
holy palsy in their hands;
hair hacked from heads—
like fundamentalists.

John, not Judas, is the villain,
with the wide-boy look
of a London stockbroker,
or an addict with a haul
of stolen goods in his trunk.
Simon is a bored professor.
Andrew, the old communist,
hauls a cross to the revolution.

Jesus—sensible, dull—
apologises for these guys
in polite company,
secretly understanding
why no girls ever joined the gang.

Journey

The sea is a glass companion.
The horizon a gateway to the sky.

We sleep below, our backs
bent against the hull, or curled
around a child.
Petrol fumes kill the old men.
I have vomited across the deck,
lightheaded and praying
for fresh air.

In the morning, the dead
are thrown overboard, the children
take an orange,
and bitter tea. We,
a cupful of grey water,
if anything.

I recognize many tongues
though no one speaks.

We sweat what is left of our water,
and tend sandpaper mouths. Mothers
hold their babies
in the air and cry for help.

But there is no help.

For another day and night,
we move on.

Navigation

We play a game where each must sleep until we dream the sea. You shall be the fisher, I your amanuensis. You have travelled to Iceland, oiling the harpoons. My job is to mark the maps and burn them in the furnace. You say 'It requires the skill of the scuba!' I carve that into the mast. Our catch is slim, but our backs are bronze plate and peeling. I collect the scales to make paper. The journal of our voyage now reaches to eight volumes. I sew the nets; mark the Transit of Venus, the line of longitude. You sweat in the hammock, febrile, muttering 'Sailors must venture far beyond, and later return in order to stand a chance.'

Andachtsbilder

1. A fisherman's coat is an oilskin

My son the angel:
oblivious to wisdom,
awkward as a seismograph,
slips into my mistakes
like a new coat.

2. After an earthquake help others if you are able

In his bedroom everything
is as he left it:
the clothes in the wardrobe,
the books in a line
on the shelf. I feel
the not him keenly.

3. At the hospital we line up like penitents

At each station I recite
'Do not let my son die.'
I hear back the sound
of the ocean,
or is it nothing?

4. Seagulls are one of the few animals that can drink salt water

Do we know,
or do we stop ourselves from knowing
what is to come?

5. The sea in this poem represents the vast unknown

Last night I watched the ocean
nail its hands to the coastline.
I thought I saw an angel,
But it was only a gull.

Seafaring

1.

An albatross above the mast as still
as a photograph.

Air lifts a wing and pushes it forward.
The hull holds a wave at bay.

A drowning son is never heard.
The ocean a bed he stumbles into.

2.

I am afraid of this defiance.
To dream of suspension above

the ocean's falling. Palms push
the ground away. Breath

is a foothold in the sky. A cloud
is water's purchase in the sky.

I am like a cloud and a breath.
Though I believe I am neither.

3.

The oracle might have sounded so
screams; hammertones; claxons;

a language of the gods
recounted by Deep Blue.

On the horizon,
the rings of Saturn

stop the breath.
As instructed

breathe away.

Focus pulling

In the economy of flesh, shame
has no tender— it is the first thing to go

And, you know, self-flagellation, if done
correctly, provides a gravity to which loose
bodies accrue. So, the calculation

arrives unbidden—a balance of junky
cunning: first make 'em weep, then
see what's in it for you.

Flight

In the space between
hairline and left eyebrow
Yuri Gagarin—Galactic Hero—
had a scar the shape
of a kerbstone's kiss
where he fell face first
after tripping from a balcony
while trying to escape
Valentina Goryacheva
who found him in bed
with a nurse called Anna.

Spaceman Bones

1. Gantry

Awake since midnight,
he had already reported in:
eggs, orange juice,
a decaffeinated coffee substitute,
a cantilever,
a butterfly.

Unable to bear his own weight,
he relied on pneumatics to stay upright,
overpowering desire,
five degrees off vertical,
looking sideways at the lane,
cold air blowing,
where his legs were joined.

2.. Quantum

Observations have revealed that I be and be not—
Schrödinger's Hamlet—apparent when noticed, otherwise
assumed to confirm the Standard Model.

Additionally, outrageous fortune is no longer available in
arrow form, but appears as a thousand hairline slits up the
skin of your arms, like a phase experiment, or an attempt
to map some reptilian forebear.

Ophelia,
when does love act as a particle,
and when as a wave?

Look how infinite I am.

3. Dear Rosa Luxemburg

Rosa, the 6th astronaut on the moon died today.
It was the incrementalism. Each morning
he woke up to check he was still.
Sloughing off ambition, he started
by telling himself to remember
it was a dream,
every day, in every way.
every day
in every way.

The chapel astronomer

The end of things might be this room of stone orange from the imperfect coloured glass no bigger than a sheet of newsprint left lying on the wall. One can see hands cut and laid the flagstones rubbed away by centuries of leather clad feet. And I am thinking of my boy and how these one thousand, ten thousand, one hundred thousand pairs of hands and eyes have made this room a living place of generations for me and for him. There is something in that—the humility of life. Please. Please. Put eyelets in the sky for his stars.

Acknowledgments

I'd like to thank Martin Dolan for casting his eye over this manuscript and editing it with care and attention. I also extend my thanks to Paul Munden, Paul Hetherington, Owen Bullock, Niloofar Fanaiyan, and Monica Carroll for offering their time and advice on various iterations of this collection, or the poems contained within, and for offering support and guidance in the world of poetry.

Thanks to Paul Hetherington and Jen Webb for chiselling the space out for creativity and writing (in a university of all places!) and including as many people as possible within it. It was fun while it lasted. Thanks to Katie Hayne and Caren Florance for their support and friendship. And to Lisa Brockwell and Penelope Layland who, along with Martin, have offered enormous support and guidance at Recent Work Press and beyond.

I am deeply grateful to Penelope Davie for her support under trying circumstances, and to Ned for all that you are.

Sue Way and David Nethercote, thank you for reading with such attention and offering enormously valuable advice.

And to the larger poetry community of Canberra—inclusive; fun; engaging; talented, and welcoming. I thank each and every one of you selfless, loving saints.

I'm very grateful to the editors of the following where poems in this collection (or versions of them) have appeared: *Axon*; *Cordite*; *Rabbit Journal*; *Western Humanities Review* (US); *Westerly*; *Found Poetry Review* (US); *foam:e*; *Text*; *Gendai-shi-techo* (JPN); *The Canberra Times*; *Verity La*, and *The Australian Prose Poetry Anthology*.

www.ingramcontent.com/pod-product-compliance
Lightning Source LLC
Chambersburg PA
CBHW020331010526
44107CB00054B/2072